Smart guide to becoming a medical representative...

Penny Dhanjal

Published 2010 by arima publishing

www.arimapublishing.com

ISBN 978-1-84549-446-9

© Penny Dhanjal 2010
Revised second edition

Printed and bound in the United Kingdom

Typeset in Palatino Linotype 11/14

arima publishing
ASK House, Northgate Avenue
Bury St Edmunds, Suffolk IP32 6BB
t: (+44) 01284 700321

www.arimapublishing.com

Contents

1.**Introduction**

You just have to take a look at the back pages of the appointments section of the Daily Telegraph on a Thursday, to see how many jobs are available in medical sales.

The medical sales field is a very popular option as it offers excellent salary potential, great benefits, flexibility, opportunity for growth and frequently the use of a company car.

The pharmaceutical industry is amongst the largest most stable and one of the fastest growing industries in the entire world. The UK Pharmaceutical industry employs approximately 60,000 people, although a vast majority are in Research and Development. In the UK medical professionals and pharmacists are responsible or the sale of drugs, which therefore opens up a huge area of opportunities for people wanting careers in sales, management and marketing.

On average it takes around 10-12 years and £550 million to develop a new medicine, with no guarantee that the medicine will become a commercial success.

According to the ABPI the value of the UK pharmaceutical industry exports in 2005 was £12.2 billion. Pharmaceuticals are one of Britain's leading manufacturing sectors bringing in a trade surplus of £3.4 billion in 2004.

The top pharmaceuticals in 2004 included Pfizer, GlaxoSmithKline, Sanofi-Aventis, Johnson and Johnson, Merck and Co, Novartis, Astra Zeneca, Roche and Bristol Myers Squibb.

Over the last decade or so the number one problem facing the representative has been gaining access to prescribers and influencers. Health care professionals are increasingly coming under pressure from all aspects of their jobs. Therefore battling for time with a health care professional is becoming increasingly difficult making the race to see your customer a competition with all the other distractions.

If you couple this with the increasing level of competitor products, increasing generic prescribing, NHS changes and cost cutting, the role of the medical representative can be a tough.

On average the cost of getting a new representative, selected, trained and out on the road, with car and everything else for a year, can cost the company an estimated £200,000 per representative. It is no wonder that companies want to make sure they get it right from the start.

The NHS is continually changing therefore the industry needs to change with it. Keeping on top of the changes is the sign of a smart company and an even sharper representative.

2. **The role of the medical representative**

Medical representatives are the key contacts between the pharmaceutical industry and the medical profession. They have the responsibility of promoting their companies major products directly to GP's and hospital doctors. They do this via face to face meetings or medical presentations at various types of meetings.

All representatives tend to work what is a called a *'territory'*. A territory is your area, or you and your territory team area. As sometimes companies have double manned territories rather than single manned territories.

The territory size, geography etc varies according to companies. The role of the medical representative is ever evolving with the evolving NHS. Some companies do not call the role sales representative any more; it can often come under the title of 'Territory account manager', 'Key account manager' etc

The day to day work of the representative tends to be target based around, sales, call rates and other objectives set around individual personal development plans.

Personal development plans tend to be the way of reviewing employee performance in most companies. They are often set around key competencies that the company are hoping the representative displays, and also around the key sales objectives set for that particular year. They are the way most companies also decide upon your pay reviews.

The image of the product and the company that a doctor forms is directly related to the degree of professionalism exhibited by the medical representative. This position therefore demands a high level of integrity and commitment to the company and its products.

Two things to remember about the role are:

1. The more you put in to the job, the more you get out.
2. Two days are never the same, there is so much variety everyday that makes the job even more appealing to people.

Organisation and Planning

Most GP's /Hospital doctors have an appointment system for seeing medical representatives. As so many other companies are trying to see the same customers, it is essential for the medical representative to be well organised and planned in advance.

By careful planning, a medical representative, will see a mix of doctors, nurses and pharmacists every day.

Those seen only by appointment and those seen without appointment but at an allocated time, this means very good record keeping of all customers is an essential skill.

A day in the life of a GP medical representative

➢ 8am +   Early morning appointments, spec calls, Card dropping. Get to as many surgeries as possible to either try and see customers then and there or arrange to try and come back later

➢ 10am +   Interviews with GP's. In these two hours. You will probably see between 3 and 5 GP's. Surgeries tend to be finishing, and all companies are bust trying to see the prescribers. Be warned it's a very busy few hours.

➢ 12.00 +   Lunch/Meetings. The meeting will entail standing on your feet and giving a presentation to the GP's in the surgery/ or Dr's in the hospital. Normally these days this is by using a company prepared slide presentation on power point. Sometimes you may have a flip chart desk presenter.

➢ 2pm +   Hospitals/ Pharmacist

➢ 4.30-5.30pm +   Home/ Admin. This will involve reporting all calls made responding to emails and requests. You may also have to speak to your manager, and most importantly plan your next day and rest of your week.

- ➤ 7.30pm+   Occasional evening meetings. This will be a meal and a promotional presentation either by you or by an invited speaker.

Be warned there is a lot of driving back and forward and around on your territory, good effective planning can minimise this, but your car is your office, so you best start getting to like being in it.

The Sales Call (see sales process in more detail later)

The sales call with GP's usually lasts between five and fifteen minutes. During this time the medical representative will discuss 2 or 3 of the company's products. The products, and their order of discussion are determined by the marketing strategy, and it is important that this strategy is followed and that a consistent message is delivered by each representative to the medical profession.

This sales call is a 2 way process where the medical representative finds out about the doctors needs and current prescribing in a particular therapy area. Then the representative aims to explain how his/her product can help answer the doctor's needs.

A high degree of technical knowledge of the disease area and the treatments available to the doctor is necessary. This knowledge is essential not only for answering any questions the doctor has, but also it will help give the representative credibility to recommend a change in the doctors prescribing habits.

The call will end with the representative asking for a commitment from the doctor to prescribe his products. At the next call the representative will discuss the results the doctor has achieved with the product and further commitment to increase usage will be gained.

Training and Development of medical representatives

Most of the major pharmaceutical companies offer extensive induction programmes to help train new representatives. This may be made up of many components, including;

1. Distance Learning (usually sent out prior to the candidate joining the company) this may include general disease area and product information.
2. 'In House' training (can last any time between 2-6 weeks). This training usually concentrates on the following:

   ❖ Technical data
   ❖ Selling skills
   ❖ Group selling skills
   ❖ Role Play
   ❖ Business Planning
   ❖ Admin requirements

3. Field Training- this is an ongoing process, it allows the representative to practise his/her new skills with a trainer or regional business manager (RBM) guiding or helping him.

Refresher courses/ updates/ frequent training and development courses may be held. The representative can expect monthly field visits from his/her RBM. This will be a day where the RBM can assess the representative's performance in front of customers, but will also allow the RBM to catch up on any territory issues affecting the representative.

Qualifications needed to get a career in medical sales.

A lot of companies look for graduates, preferably in life sciences.
However business/ law/ other degrees are acceptable. A lot more nurses are now entering the profession, their real understanding of patients and their insight into illnesses brings a new set of skills to the profession. A nurse also brings along respect from his/ her fellow medical professionals.

The key qualification needed is the ability to communicate and the drive and determination to succeed in what is a very competitive environment.

Candidates need to be of smart appearance and need to be able to demonstrate the personal qualities that are necessary to be successful.

The key personal qualities you need are:

- ❖ Ability to stay focussed
- ❖ Positive attitude
- ❖ Work hard ethic
- ❖ Organised
- ❖ Team player
- ❖ Keen to learn
- ❖ Ambition
- ❖ Drive
- ❖ Build up strong and trusting relationships
- ❖ Enthusiastic
- ❖ Work under pressure..

3. <u>Types of Sales Job In the pharmaceutical Industry</u>

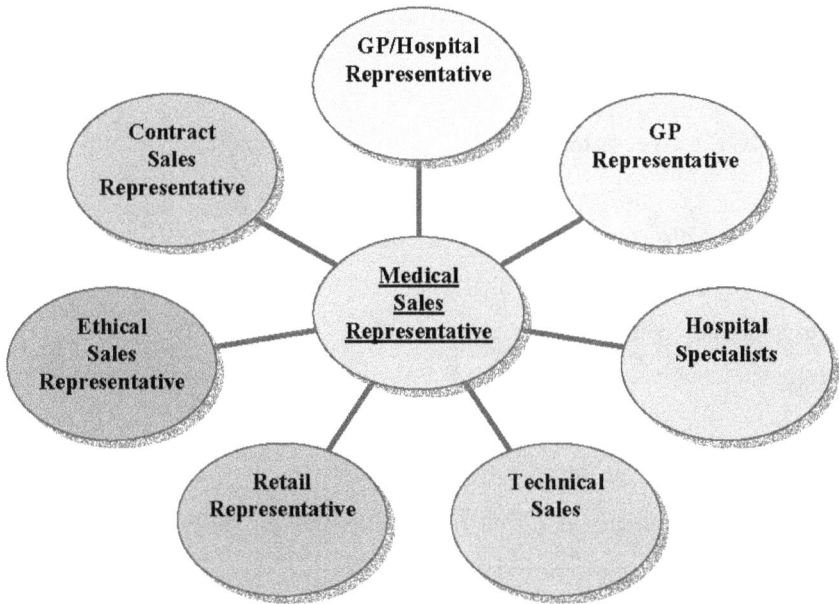

Types of sales jobs in the industry

The sales roles within the pharmaceutical industry are varied, it is important to distinguish between what you are looking for when searching for a job.

Ethical Sales

These roles normally involve working for companies selling prescription medicines or medicines which actually have been through the research and development pipeline with that company.

The types of roles include;

- **GP representatives**

These involve selling to GP's, practice nurses, pharmacists and primary are trusts.
The average content of the day involves;

- ❖ Selling to customers either on a one to one basis, or by meetings.
- ❖ Administration....this will include your daily admin, business planning, journey planning, setting pre call and next call objectives and computer work.
- ❖ Driving between customers.

These day's companies offer very flexible options to fit into people life styles. This means you can have full time, part time and term time roles.

- ❖ Part time medical representatives- working times are approximately 8am-1/2pm.Usually in primary care and may involve a small amount of evening work.

❖ Full time medical representatives- usually in primary care, working time are approximately 8am-5pm, with some evening work occasionally.

- **GP/Hospital representatives**

This involves selling to GP's and hospital customers. Again this may come with flexible working time options as above, however it is dependant on what the company wants to offer.

- **Hospital Specialists**

These representatives are 100% dedicated to the hospital setting. They will tend to visit all customers involved with their key hospital account. Selling to all those who are associated with either prescribing the medicine, being able to influence decisions e.g., nurses on wards and in the communities. Some companies have dedicated teams for particular therapy areas like diabetes, mental heath and neurology.

- **Technical Sales**

Usually involving some sort of equipment or device, this may need technical detail when selling. This role would require being able to use the equipment easily and being able to take orders directly. More of a key account manger, the geographies usually tend to be bigger for these representatives

- **Retail Representatives (OTC)**

This role may vary within a company, if a company has a lot of over the counter (OTC) products then they may have a sales force just dedicated to seeing Pharmacists/Wholesalers etc. However if a company only has 1 or 2 OTC products this may then be the responsibility of the local GP representative.

For clarification OTC products do not tend to need a doctors prescription for dispensing, and are quite often cheaper than an average prescription. They also tend to be advertised direct to the public via TV and Magazines. E.g. cough syrups, Hay fever tablets.

This role will involve a lot of negotiating with pharmacists, who as business men/women want to get the best deal they can. Sometimes it may involve brief training of the counter staff, and help with point of sale display merchandise, window displays etc.

- **NHS operations**

In different companies these representatives are termed differently some are called PCDM (Primary care development managers), and sometimes they may be called HDM (Health care development managers). The role is looked at quite highly and involves key discussions with customers at Strategic health authorities and primary care trusts. They tend to have to have a more strategic overall approach to the overall business in an area. This role is fast developing as the NHS changes, and it becomes more and more difficult to launch new drugs a lot of emphasis is being placed on Market Access. It is important to be aware of what market access is about.

In summary it is an awareness of the implications a drug can have on the wider healthcare market, considering the impact a new drug will have on a changing healthcare market, ensuring your company provides a positive healthcare environment to support the uptake of your product and finally it is important your company communicates the 'value' of your product in a way that appeals to all areas of the healthcare market.

Contract Representatives

There are specific companies that offer the opportunity to work as contract sales representatives. The most popular companies being; Zenopa, In2Focus, Ashfield and Royce.

These sales companies tend to offer a choice of teams you can work for depending on their vacancies.
The two types of teams are;

- Dedicated sales team
- Syndicated sales team

Dedicated Sales Team

Work in partnership with a contract company over a prolonged period of time, eg.6 months/12months.
The products they tend to sell belong totally to the company they are working for.
This type of arrangement gives you the advantage of working on a definite contract, and also offers you an opportunity to gain a wide range of experiences in different therapy areas. So if you want to then decide to apply for head count role, you can choose which area you

enjoy the best. Otherwise you can continue with one of the dedicated teams as it continuously offers you a variety.

Syndicated Sales Team

These tend to be managed after by the contract company. The advantages include;

- ❖ Varied product and therapy area knowledge
- ❖ Variety with little chance of boredom

4. <u>Shadowing</u>

When you first come into the industry and apply for a job, one of the first questions a recruitment company or any interviewer will ask you is…' *have you shadowed a medical representative?'* This is a vital step that you need to have achieved before applying for a job in the industry.

Obviously if you have been in the job already this does not apply to you. However this is a vital step and all new interview candidates will be asked about this.

An important point to note is, try not to just shadow one representative, shadow a few to give you experience of different therapy areas, different styles and allows you to learn about how to deal with different customer reactions.

The ways to get the shadowing experience are listed below.

1. **Network……**If you know someone already in the industry ask if it is possible to spend a day with them. Often people know of a friend of a friend so make use of the connection. Networking is a huge advantage in getting into medical sales because most firms advertise when they are unable to fill them by word of mouth.

2. **Doctors Surgery**...Talk to your local GP or practice manager. Tell them you need to shadow a medical representative. They will have many business cards for the representatives who visit them. They will be able to recommend someone. Ask for a few names to give you an example of a few types of areas of work, e.g.; GP only, GP/Hospital, GP/Nurses or GP and pharmacy. You could also ask the practice manager if they need someone to help on a voluntary basis with any work for a short period of time, in that way you can also be introduced to medical representatives as they come to visit.

3. **Retail Pharmacy**....Have a chat to your local retail pharmacy. All pharmacists know Medical representatives, if you tell them what you are after they may be able to help in the same way as above. If you time it right, you may even meet a representative while your there.

4. **Postgraduate education centre**............Most hospitals have educational facilities for their staff. Normally a postgraduate centre will have a library and lecture rooms, where staff go to revise for exams, attend lectures or for their continuing professional development meetings. The representatives tend to sponsor educational meetings in these centres. If you seek out your local postgraduate centre manager and explain what your goal is, they may be able to help. They may suggest that you come in at a

particular time of the week, so that you can chat to some of the local representatives and possibly sort out a time to shadow them.

How to get the most out of your shadowing day.

Use the following pointers as guidelines for the day:

* Spend the whole day on the road. Part of a Medical Representatives day involves 'setting the day up'. This may involve an early start and 'dropping cards'. Make sure you experience this, as the skills involved with this element of the role are vital.

* Make lots of notes throughout your field visit. Things are always forgotten. Ask lots of questions.

* Look for opportunities to discuss Pre Call Objectives

* Look to see how any objections from customers are handled.

* How was the day planned/ why were those particular customers chosen?

* How is business targeted?

* Ask to look at their business plan; do they work actively to it?

* How is success measured in their company?

* How do you become a top performer/top bonus earner?

* Ask about effective Time management

* Show your Bragg file to the rep you're shadowing to get feedback if it's OK

*What sales structure are they using?

* How do you develop the toughness to handle rejection?

* Discuss difficult customer reactions.

*How do you determine what customers are key?

If you approach the shadowing in these ways you will gain invaluable knowledge about the role of the medical representative. You will therefore find that your journey to getting the job will be a lot easier and a lot smoother.

5. <u>Who are the customers in the NHS?</u>

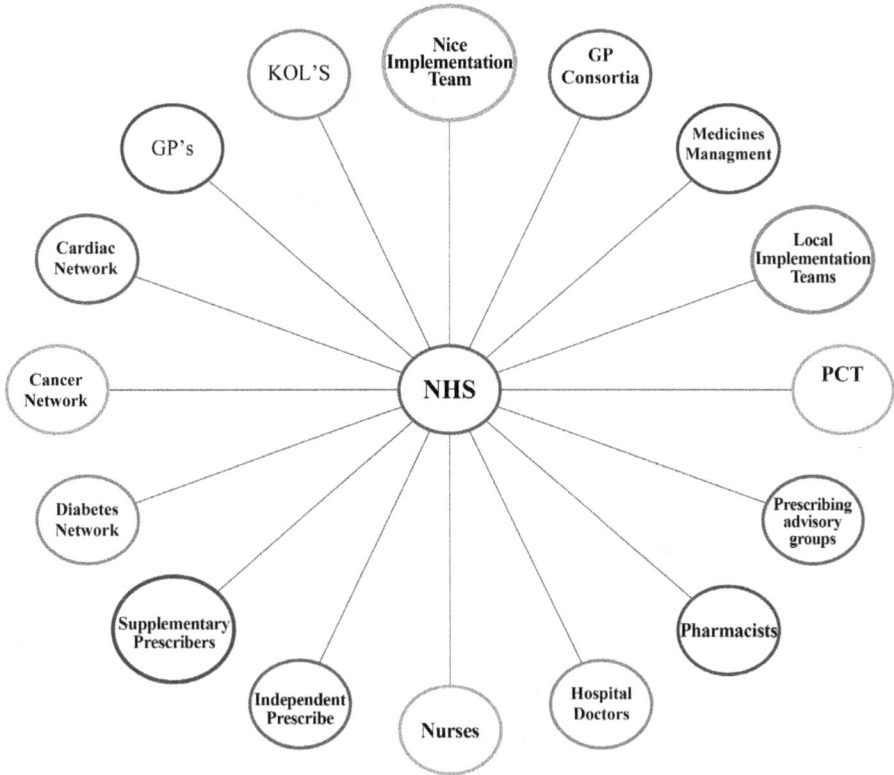

Nice Implementation Team
KOL'S
GP Consortia
GP's
Medicines Managment
Cardiac Network
Local Implementation Teams
Cancer Network
NHS
PCT
Diabetes Network
Prescribing advisory groups
Supplementary Prescribers
Pharmacists
Independent Prescribe
Hospital Doctors
Nurses

Who are the customers in the NHS

Customers will vary according to your role and marketing strategies the company have decided upon.

Primary Care Customers

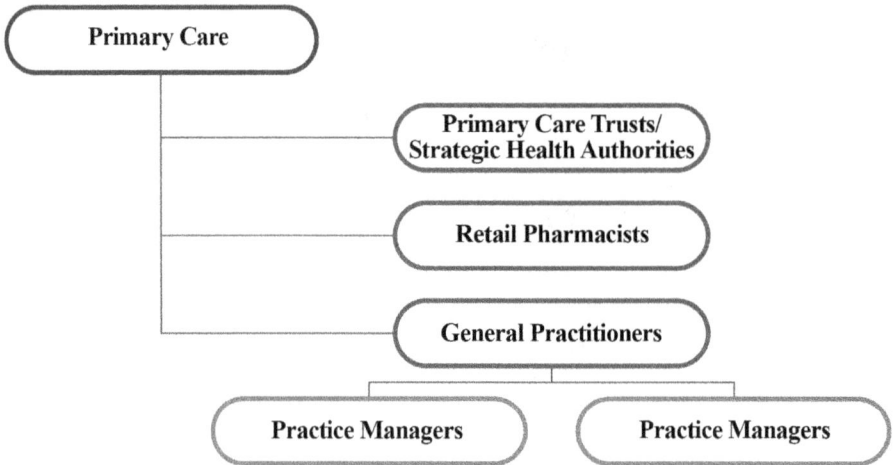

Primary Care

Primary Care Trusts/
Strategic Health Authorities

Retail Pharmacists

General Practitioners

Practice Managers

Practice Managers

Primary care customer chart

General Practitioners

These doctors look after the health of people in their local community
and deal with a whole range of health problems. They also give health
education and advice on things like smoking and diet, run clinics, give
vaccinations and carry out surgical operations.

Practice Nurses

These are a branch of community nursing based in GP surgeries and
health centres. Their role is very varied, and can include general
treatment room duties, as well as nurse led clinics in health
promotion, (e.g.   Women's   health,   coronary   heart   disease

prevention/health promotion) and chronic disease management, e.g. diabetes and asthma.

Practice Managers

Responsible for managing staff and providing HR support, developing computer and communication systems, maintaining the practice premises and keeping the finances in order. Ensure all patient services are working well.

Retail Pharmacists

The role includes dispensing prescription medicines to the public, supervising preparation of medicines, keeping a register of controlled drugs, liaising with doctors about prescriptions. Selling over the counter medicines, counselling and advising the public on the treatment of minor ailments and any advantages. They also inform on the side effects of medicines, potential interactions with other medicines and treatments. Keeping up to date with current pharmacy practice, maintaining computerised records, managing and supervising, training pharmacy support staff.. Selling healthcare and other products, such as toiletries, cosmetics and photographic items, also forms part of their role.

Primary Care Trusts..................see section on PCT's later

Secondary Care Customers

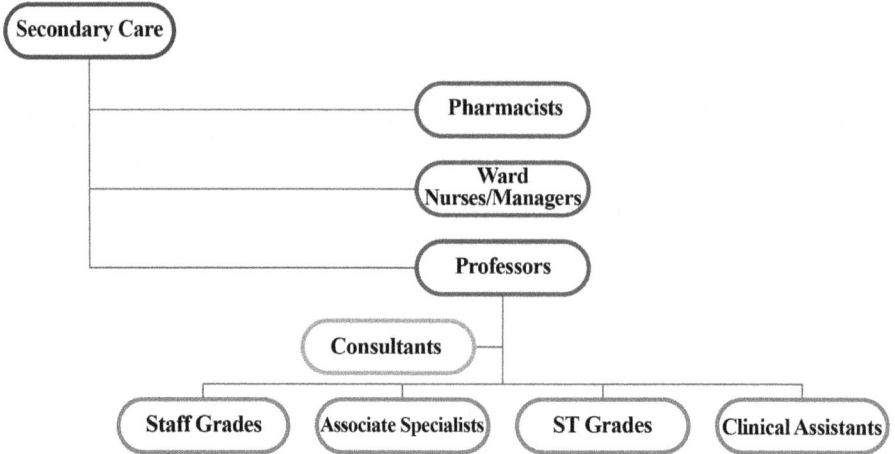

```
Secondary Care
                                    Pharmacists
                                  Ward
                              Nurses/Managers
                                  Professors
                        Consultants
        Staff Grades   Associate Specialists   ST Grades   Clinical Assistants
```

Secondary care customer chart

Hospital Pharmacists

These are experts in medication therapy, compared to nurses and physicians. Their role involves direct patient contact through ward rounds. Some hospital pharmacists are involved in teaching.

Other aspects of their role include:
-Purchasing and manufacturing medicinal products
-Monitoring and reporting patient side effects to medication
-They are responsible for the accurate dispensing and distribution of medications for inpatients and outpatients.

-Quite often they are involved in writing guidelines for drug use within the hospital, preparing bulletins and implementing hospital regulations.

-Provide information to individual ward areas on budgets and expenditure costs.

-They advise on medication, selection, administration and dosing.

Ward Nurses

Ward nurses are care providers, nurse's responsibilities include caring for all aspects of the patients care, providing patient and family education, ensuring medication is taken, teaching and training new nurses. They tend to take an active role in ward handover meetings, and often work different shift on a weekly basis, all nurses' report to a ward manger.

Professors

This is a senior academic, who holds a departmental chair. They tend to perform advanced research, conduct lectures and seminars in their field of study. They also help train young academics.

Consultants

This is a senior medic who has completed all of his/her specialist training. The time taken to become a consultant depends upon a number of factors, mainly the speciality chosen. These customers are the big prescribers.

Staff Grades/ Associate Specialists (SAS)

These doctors make up a large proportion of   hospital   doctors. The department of health estimate that approximately 12,500 doctors work in this group. These may include GP's or senior house officers who have passed their exams, and do not want to proceed any further. These doctors are usually skilled and knowledgeable in their particular speciality and are appointed based on their experience...

Clinical Assistants

Conduct new and follow up consultations, consultant leads overall management. Basically GP's are trained in a hospital speciality service, and allow the team to benefit from a generalists holistic view of patient care.

Training Grades to become a consultant physician

After completion of the medical school (MBBS/MbChB), the candidates need to do Foundation Year 1 (FY1, previously called pre-registration house officer) training that is equivalent to an overseas internship year. This leads to GMC registration for the newly qualifies doctor and is followed Foundation Year 2 (FY2).

The trainees then need to do 2 years of Core Medical Training (CT 1 and 2) at the end of which they are expected to sit and pass the full MRCP (UK) examination.

These years are followed by 5 years of Specialist Registrar training in medical sub-specialties. These Specialty Training years (ST3 to ST7) generally provide training in 2 medical sub-specialties, e.g., General and Respiratory Medicine. The ST training is 4 years for accreditation in a single medical specialty of their choice.

The trainees need to qualify a specialty examination at the completion of Specialty Training by sitting this examination anytime from ST5 year onwards. It is only after the completion of full Specialty Training and passing the exit examination that the trainee will be eligible for the Certificate of Completion of Training (CCT) that is a statutory requirement for obtaining a consultant post in the NHS. The whole process generally takes in excess of 10 years of training after MBBS/MbChB

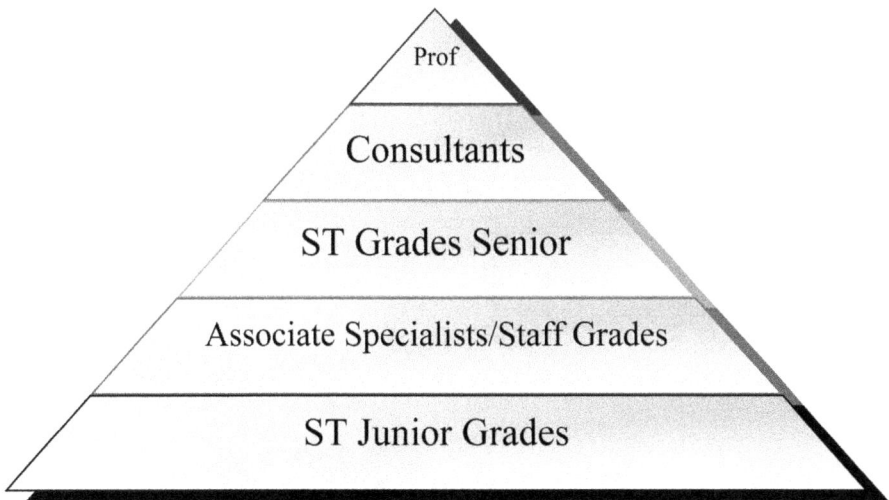

```
                          Prof

                     Consultants

                  ST Grades Senior

           Associate Specialists/Staff Grades

                  ST Junior Grades
```

Customer Hierarchy in Hospitals

6. <u>What do you need to know about the NHS?</u>

Area Prescribing Committee.

Interface between hospital and primary care and their role is to consider the cost effective entry of new drugs into both sectors. There is move away from separate formularies for PCT's and hospitals, so they may be referred to as shared care, therapy advisory groups (TAG), or interface formularies committees for these consist of local GP's hospital consultants, chief pharmacists, other pharmacist including pharmacy advisors.

Secondary Care

This is known as acute healthcare and can be either elective care or emergency care. Elective Care is planned specialist medical care or surgery after a referral from a primary care or community care health care professional like a GP.

Acute Trusts

There are 167 acute NHS trusts and 58 mental health NHS trusts, which oversee 1,600 NHS hospitals and specialist care centres.

Foundation Trusts

This is a hospital trust with financial independence. These trusts have greater freedom to manage their own affairs and improve services. The purpose of the trusts is to devolve power and responsibility to a more local level, give accountability to stakeholders including NHS patients and staff and support patient choice. High performing NHS trusts are eligible to become foundation trusts. The first foundation trust was created in 2004 there are currently 129 of these trusts across England.

More information on this is available at www.dh.go.uk

Care Trusts

Care Trusts work both in health and social care, they carry out a range of services including social care, mental health services, and primary care services.

Mental Health Trusts

NHS mental health services trusts provide mental health care in England and are overseen by the local PCT. There are 58 mental health care trusts across England providing health and social care services for people with mental health problems.

Monitor

Monitor regulates the NHS foundation trusts, making sure they are well managed and financially strong so they can deliver excellent healthcare for patients.

Currently there are 40 NHS foundation trusts; monitor gives a risk rating to each trust.

Visit www.monitor-nhsft.go.uk for more information.

Primary Care Trusts

Primary care trusts are accountable to their respective strategic health authority. They consist mainly of GP's and include other primary care health professionals. See Diagram 2.

PCT's will control up to 80% of the health spending of the local population and will be actively involved in commissioning health services locally.

There are currently 151 primary care trusts in England, 6 of which are Care Trusts. The number of Strategic Health Authorities in 2010 is 10 which have reduced from 28 a few years ago. The new SHA aim is to be more strategic and deliver stronger commissioning functions, including developing plans for improving healthcare locally, making sure health services are of a high quality and standard, increasing the capacity of services to meet the increasing demands and finally they ensure national stratergies are implemented locally.

NICE

Is an independent organisation responsible for providing national guidance on promoting good health and preventing and treating ill health.

NICE produces guidance in 3 areas of health;

Public health, health technologies and clinical practice. NICE produces formal advice for NHS clinicians and managers in England on the clinical and cost-effectiveness of new and existing medicines, diagnostic and surgical procedures.

Note: Read up on local guidelines organisations, up and down the country which can be influential:

LDNDG- London New Drugs Group is a group of pharmacists and key clinicians who review and produce guidelines on new medications.

RDTC-Wolfson Unit in Newcastle produces guidelines after reveiew of new medications.

GMMMG- Greater Manchester Medicines Management Group works to identify and advise on the appropriate use of medications across Manchester.

SMC- Scottish Medicines Consortium- their role is to provide advice to the NHS boards and their Area Drugs and Therapeutic Committees across Scotland about the status of new drugs. Quite often in Scotland if the drug is not approved by SMC it cannot be used.

AWMSG-All Wales Medicines Strategy Group brings together NHS clinicians,
Pharmacists, healthcare professionals, academics, health economists, industry representatives and patient advocates to provide advice on strategic medicines management and prescribing to the Minister for Health & Social Services.

Medicines Management

Medicines management ensures rational prescribing, e.g., patients do not continue on repeat prescriptions if they have stopped taking their medication. This then saves a lot of waste and improves patient healthcare. Medicines management collaborative are made up of hospital pharmacists, pharmaceutical advisors and primary and secondary care representatives.

National Service Frameworks

These provide national standards and target milestones with the aim of improving levels of care and removing unacceptable regional and local variations in services.
Frameworks exist for Cancer, Coronary Heart Disease, Diabetes and Mental Health.

```
                    ┌──────────────────┐
                    │      BOARD       │
                    │    Non Office    │
                    │   Members-lay    │
                    │      chair       │
                    │  Office Members  │
                    └──────────────────┘
```

Chief Executive	Finance Director	Locality/ executive managers	Managers

Executive

15+ members

Chief Executive	GP's Rx Lead Clinical Lead GP Clinical Governance Lead	Prescribing advisor	Implement-ation team lead	Nurses	2 + social service representati ves

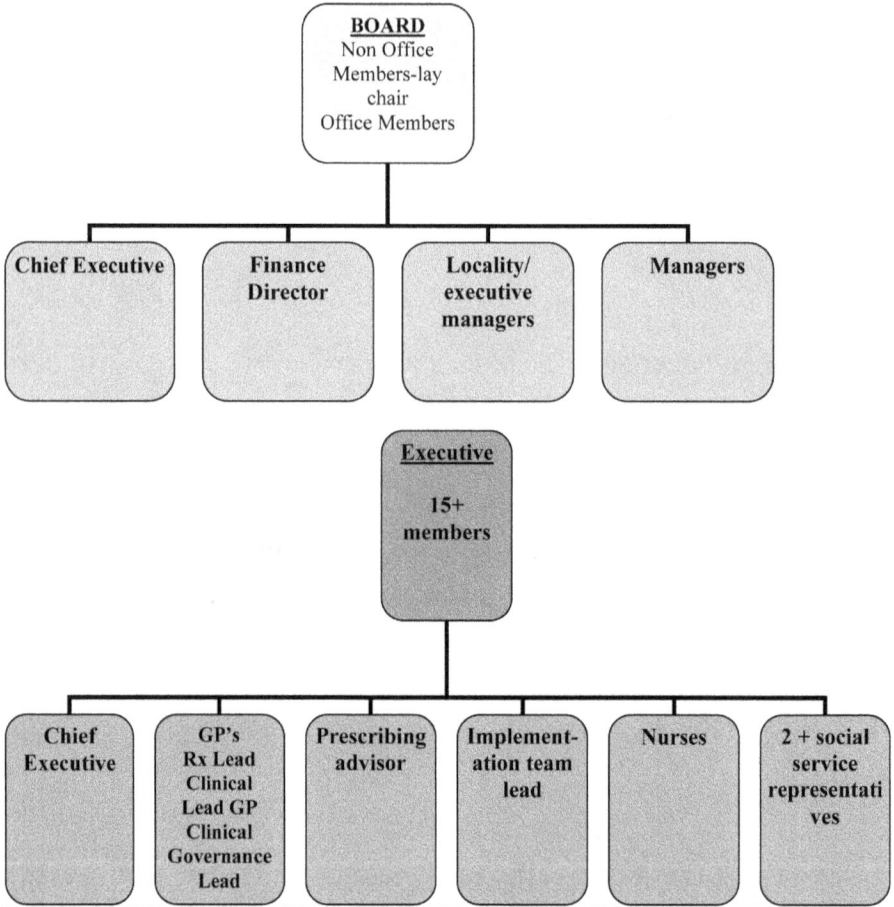

PCT Structure

Supplementary Prescribing

Diagnosis is the responsibility of an independent prescriber like a doctor or a dentist. However the supplementary prescriber will share the responsibility of writing the patient's clinical management plan.

The Health and Social Act 2001 allows for prescribing of prescription only medicine by healthcare professionals other than doctors, dentists .i.e. nurses (including health visitors and midwife and midwives and pharmacists)

Practice Based Commissioning

Practice Based Commissioning (PBC) provides an opportunity to empower clinicians and align the responsibility, accountability and authority at a level where it can be most effective in order to improve patient care in their particular community. The PBC Directed Enhanced Service (DES) applies to general practices in the UK. Within each PCT practices involved in PBC have formed clusters.

Information on the PBC clusters is available from www.nhis.info

GMS

Arrangements that apply for majority of GP's, contract between secretary of state for health and a GP within a specific practice. The contract commits the GP to provide specified services in a particular area.

PMS (Personal Medical services)

These are opportunities for GP's nurses and community trusts to test different ideas for delivering GMS; they tend to focus on local service problems and aim to bring about improvements. PMS contracts are negotiated locally with the PCT.

QOF

Quality and outcomes framework is a component of the new GMS contract for general practices, introduced from 1ˢᵗ April 2004.

QOF rewards practices for provision of quality care, and helps to find further improvements in the delivery of clinical care.

Practice participation in QOF is voluntary. QOF measures practice achievement against a range of evidence based clinical indicators covering practice organisation and management

The individual practices then score points accordingly to their levels of achievement.

The 4 domains covered by QOF include;

1. Clinical Domain
2. Organisational Domain
3. Patient experience Domain
4. Additional Services Domain

Consultant Contract

This aims to properly reward consultants so that more NHS patients benefit from their time and skills.

It aims to help NHS organisations collaborate with the profession to support service improvements and help improve doctors working lives.

Payment by Results (Pbr)

This aims to provide a transparent, rules based system for paying a trust. It aims to reward efficiency, support patient choice and diversity and encourage activity for sustainable waiting time reductions. The system will ensure a fair and consistent basis for funding hospitals.

Pharmacy Contract

Introduced in April 2005, aimed at community pharmacy, the new contract allows pharmacists to be able to provide more services. The new pharmacy contract has 3 levels of service provision;

1. Essential
2. Advanced
3. Enhanced

Essential and advanced services form part of the national contract with agreed standards.

Enhanced services are commissioned by PCT's to reflect local needs.

Agenda for Change

This is the new national pay terms and conditions system. It will seek to introduce new pay bands and harmonised terms and conditions for NHS workers.

Patient Group Directions (PGD)

These are written instructions for the supply or administration of medicines to groups of patients who may not be individually identified before presentation for treatment.

Drug and Therapeutics Committees (D & T)

These committees are responsible for the introduction of new medicines by the hospital. They play a role in determining new policies for drug usage. These are very important people for new reps to see especially if there are new drugs or indications to be launched.. The group tend to meet monthly or every two months, and the group is composed of a mixture of consultants and pharmacists.

Other Customers

Private Hospital

A private hospital is owned by a company and is privately funded, by payment for medical services or by insurers.

This is an ever increasing area of healthcare in the UK, as people struggle to cope with waiting lists to be seen by NHS consultants or have an operation. There are many private healthcare institutions up and down the country they include;

BUPA, Priory, BMI Healthcare, Nuffield, Huntercombe, St Andrews hospitals, Spire Hospitals and Cygnet Healthcare.

Worth paying attention to if you get job in the industry. These hospitals offer another avenue for sales. They often have pharmacy departments, and depending on the hospitals may or may not have the restraints that the NHS hospitals have due to funding.

Prison Network

You may not think this as an obvious place to go and visit, but my questions to you is, "don't need prisoners need medications?"

Though this is not a big avenue of sales, and the market is fairly capped, it is a good little top up to be aware of. And most areas have a prison on them, some have more than 1. Bigger prisons have a prison pharmacy, and visiting consultants or GP's come to do sessions every week.

For more information on where the prisons are around your area its worth visiting Her Majesties Prison service website, they have a map of all the establishments there.

***************************HOT OFF THE PRESS***************************

In July 2010 changes to NHS financing and structure have been launched by the government. In their new white paper entitled 'Equity and Excellence: Liberating the NHS'.

The aim of the government is to move the central control of power to patients and professionals.

The governments aim over the next 4 years is to reduce spending in the NHS by 45% and to do this it aims to reduce NHS Management costs, this may include dismantling primary care trusts and strategic health authorities.

The funding of services that GP's refer their patients to will now be looked after by a *'GP Commisioning Consortia'* in partnership with local authorities. Every GP practice will be part of a consortium. The

GP consortia will take full financial responsibility by 2013 holding up to 80% of the local NHS funds.

A new *NHS Commisioning Board* will be set up to fund and oversee the GP consortia. The department of health will fund and oversee all of this.

In secondary care the model set up by foundation trusts will apply to all NHS trusts. By April 2013 all NHS trusts will have to become foundation trusts, which means they will be regulated by **Monitor** and the **Care Quality Commission (CQC)**.

7. **Selling Skills Process**

All sales calls can follow a series of stages; generally we can map out each sales call. Companies like to have a framework for all their sales representatives to use in their contacts with customers. Therefore on a manager's field visit, they will be looking for the key steps to be followed in each call. Representatives will be marked on this through a field visit report form filled at the end of a day with your manager.

Many companies have acronyms to help people remember their selling skills processes, names like,

IDEALS

General map of a sales call...

- Pre call objectives
- Gaining Interest---Opening the sale
- Find Out Needs/Wants--Probing
- Meeting Needs—Features and benefits
- Check needs are satisfied
- Closing
- Follow up
- Post Call Objectives

Pre Call Objectives

Prior to opening the medical representative needs to be:

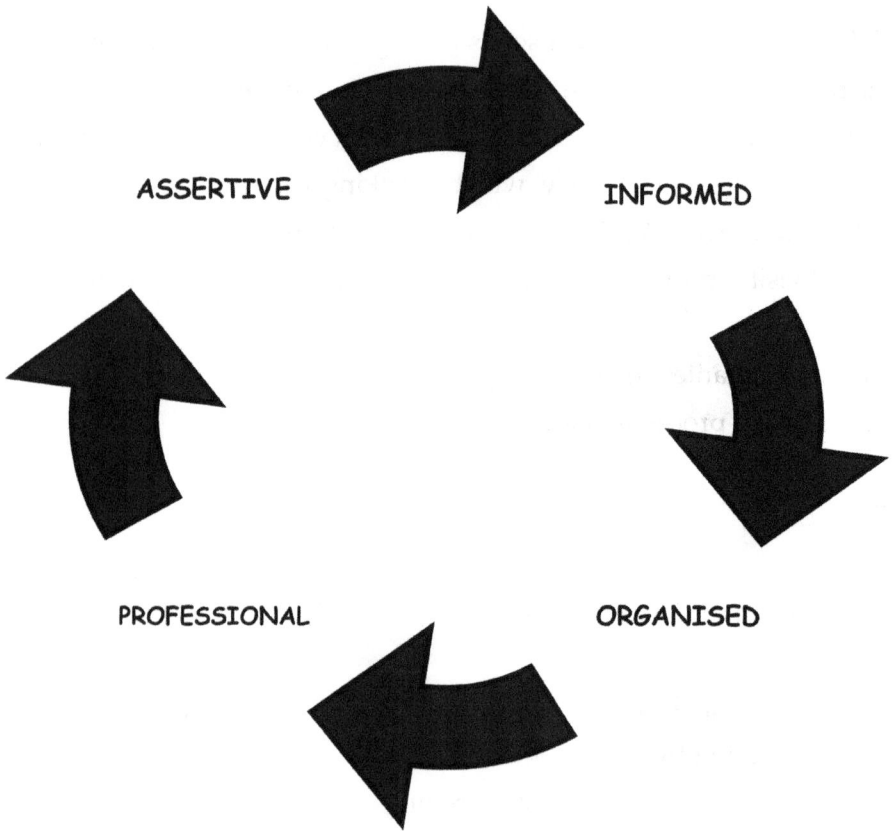

ASSERTIVE   INFORMED

PROFESSIONAL   ORGANISED

Selling Skills Process

<u>Informed</u>

- Product Knowledge
- Speciality
- Individual
- Hospital Protocol

<u>Organised</u>

- Know your call objective
- Literature
- Clinical papers
- 'On time'

<u>Assertive</u>

- Avoid Submissive behaviour
- Avoid aggressive behaviour
- Be conscious of body language

<u>Professional</u>

- Business Card
- Appearance
- Folders/Brochures
- Ethical

We must find out as much about the doctor, in order to be in a stronger position to sell. This will be from Chemists, Receptionists, Colleagues, previous details, other representatives.

Gaining Interest-Opening the sale

The first 30 seconds of a detail is the time period in which the doctor gets the first impression of the salesperson and what he/she is selling.

Therefore it is important to get the following elements right.

- o Entrance------------------be confident, relaxed and watch your body language

- o Salutation-be friendly----------- address them with correct name and pronunciation

- o Personal introduction

- o Company Introduction

- o 'Ice Breaker'--------------------'a non sales related comment'

- o General benefit statement........A statement which lets the doctor know what benefit this conversation will have for him and what it enables you to do.

The opening statement is responsible for up to 70% of the salesman's success or failure in every sale.
The opening sets the scene and gets the value of your meeting established.

Finding out Needs/Wants-Probing

A good sale depends on good interaction, it does not happen automatically. Probing questions enable us to establish and maintain dialogue with the doctor; this will enable us to have a better chance of a positive outcome.

To get information from doctors questioning skills are essential. If you cannot establish a need you cannot fill it. The two main types of questions are:

- The Exploratory question.....(Open Question)
- The Confirming question......(Closed Question)

The Exploratory/open questions should be used when establishing wants e.g. "what are your views.......?"

Begin these questions with

How, What, Why, When and Where?

A confirming question is usually answered by a 'yes' or 'no'.
The questions are usually leading questions that result in this type of reply.

Closed probes like these, lead the doctor along a certain path.

Filling Needs/Wants

A need can be split into clinical needs and personal needs.

Clinical Needs...   Efficacy
                           Side Effects
                           Convenience
                           Speed of action

Personal Needs   Comfort
                           Security
                           Social Acceptance
                           Self Esteem

A clinical need gives a reason to use a drug,

E.g., it works quickly

A personal need gives motivation to use a drug,

E.g., are other doctors prescribing it as well?

When the needs are established they can be filled by;
- Product features (tell these)

A feature is a fact.

- Product benefits (Sell these)

A benefit is how it works/helps. The benefits are quite often for both doctor and patient.

Paint patient pictures wherever possible, set the scene and make it real to the doctor.

Make sure you sell these to the doctor,

e.g. Dose is once a day
Easy to take

Effective
Good Tolerability Profile

Check Needs of Doctor are satisfied

Use questions to check that all the needs have been filled and that all questions, objections and concerns have been satisfied.

Close

1. Ask if there is any reason why Dr would not prescribe product. If the answer is 'yes' then question why, and re sell.

2. If the answer is 'no' you have an agreement.

3. Use the power of silence when asking for business

4. Be confident and determined when closing.

5. Never close if you haven't convinced the customer.

6. Summarise key benefits of the drug.

7. Ask for commitment to prescribe and organise a follow up.

   ❖ Can I call back in a few weeks to see how patient is getting on…?
   ❖ Would you like me to inform your practice nurses on any aspect of the medication?

8. Finally offer any support to the doctor and his team, invite to any key meetings, thank them and organise a repeat call back.

Post Call

Ask yourself – "What have I achieved? "- What difference has my call made to this doctors prescribing habits?

Other Selling Opportunities

Other than face to face appointments, there are group opportunities to sell, you need to have good group selling skills and keep the sales process in mind throughout.

e.g.
   ❖ Team Presentations
   ❖ Pharmacy departments
   ❖ Ward Meetings
   ❖ Journal Clubs
   ❖ Post grad meetings
   ❖ Speaker meetings
   ❖ Round Table/Peer to Peer meetings

8. __The Curriculum Vitae__

The Curriculum Vitae (CV) is usually the initial tool you will use to contact employers or recruitment companies. The value of a CV is as an initial screening tool. A poorly written CV can mean you might not get to go through to the next stage of assessment. Getting the CV right is vitally important.

Key points when preparing your CV.

- CV should be based upon achievement and what has been delivered to date
- Ideally the CV should be prepared upon a computer.
- The maximum length of a CV should be 2 sides of A4 paper
- A CV should have a strong professional visual impact. Use of bold headings, good sized margins, a good size font and adequate spacing.
- Use good quality white paper only
- Check spelling and grammar.
- If you send a CV electronically, always send a hard copy by post as well.
- Do not bind or insert the CV in a folder
- Use a confident tone and positive language
- Make it short and snappy
- Get a second opinion from someone you trust

Suggested Format

Personal Details

Your full name

Postal address and email address

Telephone number, mobile number

Date of Birth

Driving licence details, e.g. current, clean

You may want to give details on your nationality here.

Education

Give details with dates and qualifications from secondary

school onwards e.g. GCSEs, A levels

Place greater emphasis on your diploma/degree

professional qualifications.

Employment

List jobs: full time, part time and voluntary List employment with most recent first. If you have a variety of positions, give most detail for the past five

years.

Give dates in full, including months to avoid ambiguity.

Quantify your successes, and give some background on how you achieved

	them. e.g. increased sales of Product X from £10,000 to £30,000 in year 2005
Other Skills	e.g. language ability, computer skills etc
Activities and interests	Include hobbies and interests that are genuinely pursued.
Positions of responsibility	Include information on any official or unofficial organisation roles that you have taken.
References	These are optional on a CV. However if you choose to include them, one should be your current employer or tutor. Another should be a former employer. It is important to ask permission to use references, and keep them informed.

CURRICULUM VITAE

Full First Name and Surname
Address Line 1, line 2, line 3, postcode
Date of Birth

Phone number   Email

CAREER OVERVIEW

Employment....... . Overview of career to date

Employment

Company Name

Date-Present   Position

> List company role, details of role, responsibilities, achievements and geography.

Company Name

Date-Date   Position

> List company role, details of role, responsibilities, achievements and geography.

Company Name

Date-Date   Position

                       List company role, details of role, responsibilities,
                       achievements and geography.

Company Name

Date-Date   Position

                       List company role, details of role, responsibilities,
                       achievements and geography.

EDUCATION

YY-YY   School
GCSE's   Subjects

YY-YY   School
A Levels   Subjects and grades

YY-YY   Institute of Higher Education
Qualification   Degree including classification

Additional Qualifications

Other Courses

Leisure Interests

ABCD EFGH IJKL MNOP and QRST

Example CV

9. **Covering Letters**

A covering letter is necessary when responding directly to a company job advertisement or for speculative approaches to companies, but it is of less importance when applying to a recruitment company.

Guidelines for a covering letter

- Name
- Address
- Telephone numbers
- Details of job applied for
- Mention that you are enclosing a CV.
- Source of job vacancy, e.g. company website
- A brief paragraph on why you feel you should be considered for the role and why you want to work with the company.
- Include details on your availability for interview, holiday dates, conference dates.
- Address your covering letter to a specific person whenever possible
- Use good quality paper and envelopes

On the next page is an example covering letter, for someone out of university applying for a role in the industry.

Example covering letter.

J Stuart

44 The Rise

Castle Haven

Northampton

NN3 4UP

27TH January 2007

Mrs M Smith

Covex Pharmaceuticals

15 Netheredge Street

Wilmslow

Manchester

M4 1RP

Dear Mrs Smith,

My name is John Stuart and I am writing in response to your advertisement for a GP medical representative in Manchester. I enclose a CV for your consideration.

I first became interested in medical sales during a 'careers fair' at University. Since then discussion with my careers advisor, friends in the industry and my own research have confirmed my belief that this is a career which will enable me to use my interest in sales and pharmaceuticals, but also my skills in working with people both in a team and outside customers.

I am particularly interested in Covex pharmaceuticals because of the drug portfolio and the commitment made to investing into further research and development into cardiovascular medicines.

During my time as a student I have had a variety of part time and vacation jobs, all of which have required me to work as part of a team and to deal directly with the public.

I found my work at the tourist information office particularly valuable in teaching me the importance of ascertaining customer needs and providing clear and accurate responses to those needs.

I will be available for interview at any time apart from 12-24th February when I have booked a holiday. I look forward to hearing from you shortly.

Yours Sincerely

John Stuart

John Stuart

10. The Process of getting the job

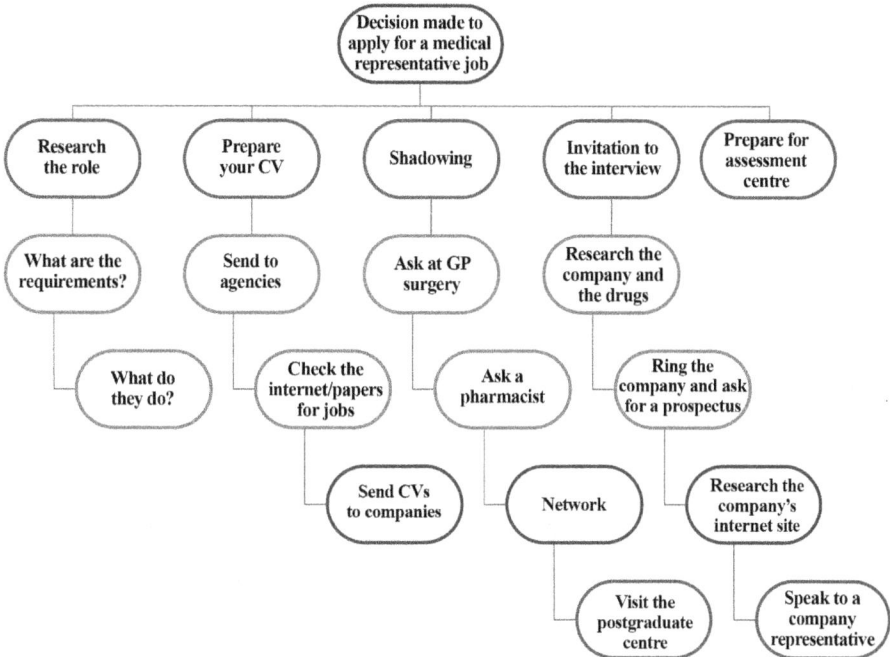

In the past each company and recruitment company varied the way they interviewed and assessed their candidates. However now there seems to be a standard process which all companies are sticking to.

These days you are more than likely going to be looking for a career in medical sales with the help of a recruitment company. Therefore the process is as follows;

- ➢ Send Your CV/ Fill application form

- ➢ Interview with recruitment company

- ➢ Selection for Assessment centre

- ➢ Possible Second Interview

- ➢ Job Offer!!!

Interviews

Getting a job has always been about getting through an interview.
The interviewer is looking for you to show them that you are capable of being their Top Performing Representative.
In order to interview well you need to be well prepared and confident. The problem with most people is that they view the interview process as an interrogation process, and with that comes all the negative images.

Here are some top tips to get you through the whole process.

- ❖ Preparation is essential if you want to succeed at an interview. Ensure you fine tune your knowledge of the employer. Aim to arrive early to the venue. Practise your interview and answers to possible questions before the interview. Try and practice relaxation and visualisation techniques. This will help to calm your nerves and focus you on the positive end result you want from the interview. Make sure you cover all the bases, find out the interview format… will there be one interviewer or a panel of interviewers.

❖ Know your numbers, what are your sales? Sales versus target, market share, call rates etc. Use your information in the bragg file to support this.

❖ If you are supplying a CV make sure you know your own CV. Try and thoroughly memorise it and can support every line in the CV.

❖ Listen to all questions carefully, and think before you answer. Remember that interviewers are trying to find out if you can do the job, and how you will fit into the team/company.

❖ Know your strengths and weaknesses; you are almost certain to be asked questions on these. Know your strengths and always try to relate them to the position you are applying for. If you are asked about a weakness, remember to try and reframe them as strength. Show that you are overcoming a weakness, and that you have learned. Another way to overcome a weakness is to pick a weakness that is really strength. If for example you're interviewing for a job in an organisation that you know is hard charging and unforgiving of average performance, you could say 'one *of my weaknesses is that I tend to be inpatient with people who aren't willing to pull their full weight and give 110%*'. In this case your 'weakness' may help you get your job.

- ❖ Remember that if you have been fired, be honest about it. Try not to be bitter, so many people have been laid off through no fault of their own.

- ❖ Be clear where you want to go in the job. A standard question is *'where do you want to be five years from today?'* The industry is changing so much, so a possible response could be '*I plan to be become qualified I every phase of this industry'*

- ❖ Be realistic about what your worth, and when it comes to salary, stand your ground.

Your first interview will be with the recruitment company, a consultant from the company will run through the interview based on what you have put down on your CV or application form. Treat this seriously as this is a screening interview as this will let the recruitment company know whether you are what their client companies are looking for. Quite often the consultant can guide you on areas you can strengthen in preparation for your next interview. Be clear about what you are after in terms of role and location.

11. <u>Competencies and competency based questions</u>

Analytical Thinking

The ability to understand problems and situations by breaking them down into their component parts and analysing them logically.

Possible questions asked

- How do you monitor and evaluate your success at work?
- Tell me about when you had to identify the key cause of a problem.

Business Awareness

Demonstrates understanding of the company products and market and how these compare to its major competitors
Actively seeks information on the aspects of the industry or market place which impact upon our own area of work.

Possible Questions asked

- What do you consider to be the main issues facing the pharma industry today?
- Give an example of where you have spotted a good business opportunity.

Communication

Presents facts logically and is sensitive to the communication needs of others. Demonstrates effective eye contact, and confident body language. Participates in meetings, communicates well at all levels and behaves assertively.

Possible Questions asked

- Describe an occasion where you correctly identified the needs of a customer.
- Describe a situation when you have had to explain a complex subject to an individual.

Decision Making

Critically evaluates numerical data and written material. Assembles all relevant facts in the decision making process. Understands the consequences of decisions. Demonstrates the effectiveness and suitability of decisions made to suit the business needs. Demonstrates a logical analysis of problems.

Possible questions asked

- What is the hardest decision you have ever had to make?
- What scope does your current job provide for taking decisions?

Organisational Skills

Manages own time effectively to achieve targets by identifying, prioritising and scheduling tasks. Monitors, evaluates and adapts planning in order to meet customer needs, and considers alternatives. Anticipates when deadlines may not be met and makes the necessary adjustments.

Possible questions asked

- How do you deal with peaks and troughs in your workload?
- Describe a major project you have managed.

Personal Effectiveness and Creativity

Tackles problems from more than one angle, Identifies new ways of tackling problems or situations. Identifies market opportunities, applies existing expertise in new market areas. Adds value to a product, copes with pressure, keeping the ability to think clearly and stay calm.

Possible questions asked

- How would you add value to the company?
- Tell me about a creative idea you have had and how you went about selling it to others.

Persuasiveness

Persuades influences and convinces others. Anticipates likely objections and builds effective responses into the approach. Emphasises positive messages and key benefits.

Possible Questions asked

- What are your strengths in terms of influencing people?
- Give me a recent example of when you negotiated a successful sales outcome.

Self Motivation and Achievement Orientation

The basic drive to do things even better, to set and strive for challenging goals for oneself and other. Approaches challenges with energy, enthusiasm and determination to succeed.

Possible Questions asked

- What demotivates you?
- What is most important to you in your current rol

Other questions that could be asked.

- ❖ What are your biggest successes to date?
- ❖ Can you think of an example when you have worked in a successful team, what made it a success?
- ❖ Take me through how you plan your day and the week ahead?

❖ Has a customer (either internal or external), ever asked you to do something which is over and above what is expected? How did you handle the request and what was the outcome?

❖ Give me some examples of when you have been particularly motivated. What was it that got you motivated?

❖ In your previous job what did you enjoy the most? What did you enjoy the least?

❖ Why do you want to move from your current role?

❖ Think of a time when you have had to juggle various tasks at once, can you take me through how you did this?

❖ What is successful to you and why have you been successful in the past?

❖ What do you contribute to your present team?

12. Bragg File

Throughout your interview it is vital that you are able to present examples of your strengths and skills to support what you are saying. Use of a bragg file is just like a sales aid in a call with a customer, without supporting evidence, the call is no good.

Take your feedback in an organised format. Get a good file and make sure you categorise your evidence in sections so you know what you are looking for when asked.

Employers have been known to complain about candidates who root around box files of ageing yellow papers in search of 'just one more email'.

Categorise your file as follows:

❖ Certificates/Documentation these include
-Degree Certificates
-ABPI
-Other courses attended
-Driving Licence
-Possibly Passport

Have extra copies of your driving license and passport, as quite often the interviewers will require this.

❖ Feedback evidence......From internal and external customers

-Recognition letters and emails from superiors, this can include your RBM, head office staff, managing director etc
-Testimonials from customers, any letters of thanks and support
-Emails from peers also help to endorse your team player skills
-Good field visit report forms

❖ Sales/League tables......In date order   -
        Sales Vs Target
        -Market share   -
        Sales Growth   -
        Call Rate/Meeting activities

❖ Evidence.....All other evidence of your success.
        -Recent Awards
        -Winning regional incentives
        -Winning national incentives and   prizes
        -Any other incentives you have won.

Make sure you know your Bragg file, there is nothing worse than fingering through and not knowing where your evidence papers are.

13. Assessment Centres

Typically an assessment centre is when you join a small group of six to eight other candidates, probably applying for the same jobs, and who are all ready to undertake a series of assessments designed to show the watching selectors that you possess most of the personal and technical skills necessary to do the work.

This can take from a few hours to a few days. For employers the main reason for using assessment centres is so the more information they have the less of a risk they feel they are taking with individuals.

Whilst an interview is still regarded as the most traditional approach the use of a structured multiple assessment approach will provide a more accurate assessment of the candidate's suitability for the role and provide them with an opportunity to demonstrate their competence.

The benefits therefore are that the assessment centre provides a variety of assessment techniques, which are matched to the requirements of the job. The breadth of techniques is intended to ensure more comprehensive assessment and measurement of the requirements of the role.

The assessment centre approach aims to measure the following areas of competencies:

Team work with others- Behaviours that demonstrate the ability to work as part of a team, as well as the importance of networking and collaboration.

Interpersonal and Communication Skills- Behaviours that indicate sound written, verbal and non-verbal communication skills.

Organisation and planning- Behaviours that demonstrate the ability to plan and organise to ensure maximum efficiency.

Motivation and results orientation- Behaviours that demonstrate commitment, enthusiasm and the achievement of results.

Client Focus and business acumen- Behaviours that demonstrate customer care together with an understanding of the business and market place.

Technical knowledge and skills- Behaviours that demonstrate the individuals desire to learn and continually update their skills.

What can you expect?

All organisations design their own assessment centres but many of them will contain similar elements. There may be variations depending upon the company's own requirements.

It is fair to assume that they will involve you in one or more group exercises, and ask you to do a presentation. Often you will have to sit a series of aptitude tests, and generally speaking you won't have seen the back of interviews. This time around, the interviews will be more challenging and may involve a number of interviewers.

Make sure when you are called to an assessment centre, look the part, unpolished shoes, poorly ironed shirts, a suit that has seen better days will create a less than stunning first impression.

A typical example of an assessment day could be as outlined below.

Assessment Centre Day Plan

09.30   Meet other candidates. Tea and coffee,   everyone
             is looking nervous.

10.00   **I.T test.** No calculator or notes allowed. Usually
             involves Excel spreadsheet input of numbers and
             working out the means, or drafting and
             email/memo. Not as bad as it seems.

10.30   **Group discussion.** Up to six people in a group,
             they are given 30 minutes to look at a given
             scenario, and feed back their plan of action.

11.15   **Numerical Test.** No calculator allowed, but a
             scrap piece of paper can be used to work out
             answers.

11.45	**Interview.** Competency Based, may involve HR as well.
12.30	**Verbal Reasoning Test.** No materials needed for this.
13.00	**Presentation by company.** More than likely this will be done by the managing director and/or the public relations team. It will be a look at the origins of the company, its company visions and values, existing and pipeline of products and a look to the future.
13.30	**Lunch.** A good time to fuel up on that much needed caffeine.
14.30	**Presentation.** 10-15 minute presentation, which you will have pre-prepared based on a title you will have been given. There will be time after for questions on the presentation.
15.15	Tea and Coffee, feedback from other group members
15.45	Depart, more than likely exhausted but elated.

* A growing number of companies are now adding a business simulation exercise into the assessment centre programme. A business scenario is given, quite often this may be a launch of a new product,

and you will be given information on the competitor market, and demand and asked how and why you would launch the product.

Group Exercises

Assessors may be looking for very difficult attributes, typically though group exercises are designed to identify leadership skills, the ability to facilitate the group in moving forward without 'bulldozing' them into submission.

Active participation is crucial-sitting on the sidelines, rarely scores plus points. Other than that, the ability to listen, challenge constructively, input creatively and negotiate your position, are all important elements of a group exercise.

Throughout the group exercises you will be watched carefully by assessors with clipboards.

WARNING.....Beware that a lot of experienced representatives who have been on previous assessment centres are aware of what happens in a group exercise. They may storm in and take over straight away. Note that there are other ways to take control;

- Offer to take notes for the presentation at the end
- Offer to flip chart ideas as they are decided upon.

Key skills needed in a Group Exercise:

- *Is a Team Player*.....Show that you can work successfully in a team and listen to other people's points of view.

- _Confidence_..............This is vital you can not be lacking in this.

- _Communication Skills_... - you need to be articulate enough to express your views coherently.

- _Analytical skills_ - the ability to analyse a problem and identify solutions is crucial.

Examples

1. Your group exercise may be where the assessors hand you a sheet with information on a mock company which is deciding to launch a new product. The information will include trial data, market information, competitor information and company profit/loss data. From this information you may be asked to decide upon the products launch plan or launch delay, and have a robust argument for the path you choose.

Quite often in these sorts of exercises there are no right or wrong answers, however, the assessors who sit around the room watching and making notes on everyone, will be looking at your reactions, inputs, body language, interactions and logical arguments.

2. Your group is asked to take the role of a Research Management Committee responsible for administering extraterrestrial research projects in a secret location in Northern England. You have called an emergency meeting to discuss one of the projects the committee is responsible for.

The project, which is studying likely human behaviour in a colony to be established on another planet, is conducting an experiment in an astrodome. The experiment involves six international volunteers living in an astrodome. The group's only outside connection is a radio link to a research station. A call for help has been received from the volunteers; they have been trapped in the astrodome by a major escape of an inert gas which is reducing the oxygen level to a life-threatening extent.

The rescue team reports that rescue will be extremely difficult and with the equipment at its disposal, only one person can be brought out each quarter of an hour. This makes it possible (but not inevitable) that the rapidly reducing oxygen level will asphyxiate some of the volunteers before rescue can be effected. Through their radio link with the research station, the volunteers have been made aware of the dangers of their plight. They have communicated that they are unwilling to decide on the sequence in which they will be rescued. The responsibility for making this decision now rests with you- the Research Management Committee. You must decide the order of rescue.

Life saving equipment will arrive in 30 minutes at the astrodome entrance.

Each member of the group is responsible for the ultimate outcome of this emergency meeting. You may have to justify your decisions.

Presentation Exercise

The title for the presentation exercise will be given in advance of attending the assessment centre. The approximate time given to deliver the presentation will be about 15 minutes, and maybe 10 minutes for questions from the assessor after.

Make sure you spend time planning the content of your presentation, spell check all your slides.

Rehearse the presentation in front of people, and get their feedback. When practising make sure you get your timings right. Be ready for interruptions, how will you handle them? Don't be thrown off your stride!!

The presentation should be made using PowerPoint. Make sure that this is saved on to a disc, CD Rom, memory stick and ensure that it has been virus checked.

So what are they looking for?

- Structure to the presentation- a beginning, middle and an end.
- Use of AV media
- Time keeping
- Ability to handle questions
- Presentation skills
- Enthusiasm
- Lessons learned
- Knowledge of presentation subject.
- Attitude to problems
- Use of relevant examples
- Creativity to problem solving

- Monitoring systems
- Objective setting

How you come across is more important than what you say.

This is vitally important as the job you are applying for involves a large component of presenting to customers. So obviously an employer wants to make sure the employee will make an impact.
The actual message of your talk will be transmitted partly, through the words you speak. Research has shown that the message is transmitted non-verbally, by the way you present.
Your body language can make a huge difference to your presentation.

o Voice

Nerves almost always make you speak faster. Force yourself to slow down and pause between sections of your talk. Avoid mumbling.

o Eyes

Communication is always easier with eye contact. Sometimes it is difficult to talk to the audience but you must try.

o Movement

Unnecessary movement will distract the audience's attention. If you do move, move for a purpose and move purposefully.

o Hands

Use your hands naturally. If you make gestures when you talk to people, use the same gestures in your presentation. Resist the temptation to fiddle with your pen.

The presentation titles can vary from, what you will do on territory on your first 6 months to ……………..

What will you do in your first 6 months in the job?

Although this book is aimed at those looking at trying to get a job within the industry for the first time, this section may seem irrelevant at this moment in time. However this section is something you are more than likely to be asked to present about or discuss at your interview.

If you are asked to present or discuss this subject at your interview below are some tips to guide you.

'My first 6 months on territory'

- Be fully trained and up to date with all my product knowledge

- Ensure I know where all my customers are on my territory.

- Be aware of all the competitors on the territory, there sales and activities.

- Be up to date with all sales data

- Network via medical secretaries, medical staff, pharmacy and nursing staff.

- Build Relationships

- Work accounts effectively…key accounts

- Build up an appointment bank

Aptitude Exercises

These will include a numerical and verbal assessment, which will be completed on the day.

An Occupational personality questionnaire may be completed on line prior to attendance at the assessment centre.

Verbal Reasoning Tests

There are different types of verbal reasoning tests, for example you might be asked to identify the relationships between pairs of words. Many verbal reasoning tests are used to assess logical reasoning. e.g., determining the correct sequence of a set of sentences in order to test verbal analysis and comprehension. Another way to assess your reasoning is to ask you to read a passage and then evaluate several statements in accordance with the set rules.

Example Verbal Reasoning Questions

1.

> The number of accidents, which occur during the course of the working day, will never be reduced to zero, regardless of the attempts of regulating bodies. This is because all activity inevitably involves some degree of risk and luck. However, it is possible to reduce the number of occupational accidents, and one way of doing this would be to impose punitive fines on organisations within which occupational accidents occur. Whilst this will result in cases of injustice to some organisations, the overall effect for the employee, in terms of securing a safer workplace, will surely be beneficial.

1. Some accidents at work are the result of misfortune.

2. Organisations have no power to make workplaces safer.

3. Under the proposed system of fines, organisations taking safety seriously would have nothing to fear.

4. A system of fines is the best way to reduce accidents in the workplace.

A True

B False

C Cannot say

Base your answers **only** on the
information given in the passage

2.

Advertising and selling books via Internet sites is becoming more popular with traders. It costs less to publicise a book on the Internet than by traditional methods, and as books are stored in warehouses prior to being dispatched to customers, overheads are lower than those of shops. True, the price war on the Internet is likely to put pressure on royalties, with publishers demanding that they be calculated not on the cover prices of books but on the prices actually received for them. However, these discounts will be greatest on best-sellers, rather than other books.

1. The consumer demand for books sold on the Internet is increasing.

2.. The cost of placing an advertisement for a book on the Internet is less than other methods of marketing.

3.. Internet bookstores offer their biggest discounts on less popular books.

4. Writers will definitely lose money because of the nature of Internet book-selling.

A True
B False
C Cannot say

Base your answers **only** on the
information given in the passage

Numerical Reasoning Tests

As with verbal reasoning tests there are several different types of assessment, one example may be to establish the relationship between adjacent numbers that will enable you to complete the pattern. A popular form of test involves completing a series of numbers, series of letters of the alphabet, or a row of dominoes.

Another way to assess your reasoning is to ask you to make approximate calculations to specific questions by referring to a table of data, a graph or a chart.

Example Numerical Reasoning Questions

1. *The driving time for a 100 mile trip from Townsville to Cityville was two and half hours. The return trip was made by the same route but at an average speed that was about 50% faster. What was the total amount of driving time for the entire round trip?*

   A. *3 Hrs 45 mins*
   B. *4 Hrs 10 mins*
   C. *4 Hrs 16 mins*
   D. *4 Hrs 45 mins*
   E. *6 Hrs 15 mins*

2. *A manufacturing company produces a special water resistant paint with secret ingredient X. Every 150 tins of paint produced requires 14.75 litres of ingredient X.*

It costs the manufacturer £9.50 per litre to make ingredient X. One tin of paint sells at £18.99.

If the company wants to fulfil an order for 8,500 tins, what will the costs be for making ingredient X?

1. £15,3475
2. £161,415
3. £7940
4. Cannot say

Personality Questionnaires

Personality questionnaires are a standard and objective way of discovering your preferred ways of behaving and relating to other people. They allow an employer to see if you fit the behavioural requirements of a particular job. These tests are really not tests at all, even though they consist of a large number of questions that demand answers.

Personality questionnaires tell the organisation nothing about your ability but quite a lot
about the type of person you are and what you want out of life.

No organisation is weird enough to be looking for one sort of personality, so just relax and answer the questions honestly.

- There are no right and wrong answers.
- There is no time limit
- You often get a chance to talk over your 'profile' with the assessors.

Personality questionnaires are impossible to prepare for and impossible to rig. It's a time wasting exercise if you try to fake your questionnaire results, as you will become seriously unstuck, as there are internal checks of consistency built into the list of questions.

The best way to tackle these is to be positive about yourself and answer the questions positively.

Example Personality Questions

1. **In doing ordinary things are you more likely to:**

   A. *Do it your own way*
   B. *Do it the usual way*

2. **In doing do you:**

   A. *Rarely question that all will be said*
   B. *Rehearse what you'll say?*

3. **For each of the following pairs of statements, indicate which you find *most* comfortable doing or thinking:**

ensuring other people do things in the correct manner	Question:	1	appreciating the importance of those things I feel strongly about
	□ □ □ □ □ □		

| taking greater | Question: | 2 | deducing the logic |

care of other ▢ ▢ ▢ ▢ ▢ ▢ behind why things
people's happen
feelings

4. **For each of the following pairs of statements, indicate which you _enjoy_ doing or thinking most**

trying to do
something
that's never
been tried
before

Question: 3
▢ ▢ ▢ ▢ ▢ ▢

producing lots of detailed
information

forming new
theories
about things

Question: 4
▢ ▢ ▢ ▢ ▢ ▢

building a more friendly
atmosphere

5. **For each of the following pairs of statements, indicate which you think is the _worse fault._**

people
dwelling too
much on
particular
details

Question: 5
▢ ▢ ▢ ▢ ▢ ▢

people continually
changing the topic of
conversation

people taking a short-sighted approach	Question: 6	people dreaming about unrealistic ideas

After the assessment centre

On rare occasions you may be told of your fate before you leave the assessment centre. More normally, though, you will receive a letter within a week or so telling you of their decision.

If you're lucky with some of the recruitment agencies will send you a detailed report of your scores and how you were graded for the various exercises along with any notes. This is a great way to look at any areas to improve in the future. Always look at assessment centres as learning exercises; you can use this for personal self development.

However if you don't receive this feedback and don't get the job, you can phone the organisation and ask for feedback.

If you get offered a job and you don't want to accept it, immediately, write to them thanking them for he offer and let them know that you will let them know of your decision by whenever.

14. ABPI

Association of the British Pharmaceutical Industry

The ABPI is the governing body which monitors closely the activities of the Pharmaceutical industry. The way it does this is by setting up a Code of Practice.

All representatives need to take and pass their ABPI exam, within a year of being employed within the industry.

The exam is divided into two papers, one covers anatomy and physiology the other covers a specialist subject area, normally chosen by the reps company. This subject normally tends to be one that the representative has most experience selling in, so it can range from any of the following, Cardiology, mental health, dermatology or contraception to name a few.

Then aim of the Code of Practice is for the pharmaceutical industry is to ensure that the promotion of medicines to health care professionals and appropriate administrative staff is carried out in a reasonable, ethical and professional manner.

The code of practice affects every aspect of a representative's work so it is something that should be in the forefront of the representative's mind every day.

The Code of practice looks at:
- Promotion

- Calls with customers-Frequency, Length and timing
- Promotional materials
- Letters to customers
- Sponsored materials
- Gift/competitions
- Medical and educational goods and services
- Samples and stock
- Meetings-content, attendees, speakers, presentations and venue
- Hospitality and travel
- Medical and Educational Grants
- Materials
- Honoraria

The New ABPI 2008

The new ABPI Code of Practice came into effect from January 1st 2008. There is an update anticipated in 2011. What is important for you to be aware of at this stage is that the code affects a number of areas for the sales representatives. The areas involved are;

o **Frequency of visits to customers in a year**

"The number of calls made on a doctor or other prescriber and the intervals between successive visits are relevant to the determination of frequency.

Companies should arrange that intervals between visits do not cause inconvenience. The number of calls made on a doctor or other prescriber by a representative each year should not normally exceed three on average. This does not include the following which may be additional to those three visits:

- Attendance at group meetings, including audio-visual presentations and the like

- A visit which is requested by a doctor or other prescriber or a call which is made in order to respond to a specific enquiry

- A visit to follow up a report of an adverse reaction.

Representatives must always endeavor to treat prescribers' time with respect and give them no cause to believe that their time might have been wasted. If for any unavoidable reasons, an appointment cannot be kept, the longest possible notice must be given.

o **<u>Give away costs and types of give a ways</u>**

'Items provided on long term or permanent loan to a doctor or other prescriber or a practice is regarded as gifts and are subject to the requirements of this clause.

Promotional aids must be inexpensive and relevant to the recipients' work and are more likely to be acceptable if they benefit patient care. An 'inexpensive' promotional aid means one which has cost the donor company no more than £6, excluding VAT. The perceived value to the recipient must be similar"

o   **Medical Education and Grants**

It is okay for a company to help a healthcare organisation – though the support must be of benefit to patient care or the NHS or for research.

The details of the grant must be documented and recorded. Like the contracting of services from HCPs and institutions, the grant must not be seen as an inducement to prescribe, recommend, administer, buy or sell a product.

o   **Contracts with Health Care Professionals**

Each time a pharmaceutical company wants to engage the services of a healthcare professional, the details of the arrangement needs to be captured in a written agreement. This will mean a formal contract that the healthcare professional has to sign e.g. Speaker agreement or consultancy agreement. These agreements are ideally signed before the health care professional engages in the event.

This means every speaker will need to be working under a contract every time they speak at a company meeting. Or act in the capacity of chairperson.

The contract should include details about the service that the HCP is providing and the basis for the payment. The payment must be at Fair Market Value. This essentially means that two HCPs with an equivalent seniority providing roughly the same service should be paid roughly the same amount of money. There needs to be a company system of collating and storing all these documents.

Companies may also include within the contract the requirement for health care professionals to declare their work for the company.

o   **All meetings to have clear Medical Content.**

This section has been reviewed and includes extra information on hospitality as well.

'If meetings are sponsored, this fact should be declared in all relevant documentation such as invitations. The requirements are:

-Meetings must have a clear educational content.

-The venue must be appropriate; lavish or deluxe venues must not be used and venues renowned for their entertainment facilities should be avoided

-Subsistence (meals and drinks) must be secondary to the purpose of the meeting and not out of proportion.

-Hospitality must not extend to a spouse or similar unless that person qualifies in their own right as an attendee.

-Spouses or similar, unless qualified as above, must not attend the actual meeting or receive, at the company's expense and associated hospitality.

-Quizzes are not allowed at promotional meetings-as long as they are non-promotional in nature and test the learning gained at the meeting and as long as there is no prize

o   **All representatives must have passed the ABPI examination. There are no exemptions from the exam. This exam can be sat as a final exam or depending on your company they may ask you to sit it in a modular system.**

'All company personnel involved in promotion or in the preparation of promotional material must be fully conversant with the Code, representatives must take the ABPI examination within one year of commencing employment as a representative and must attempt the exam within one year of commencing their first employment.'

15. <u>Rewards of the job</u>

There are lots of rewards to go for; all companies have incentives to reward their high performing representatives.

Most companies tend to have the following in some form:

- ❖ Bonus Schemes based on sales vs. target or activity
- ❖ High flyers clubs, e.g. 'All Stars'
- ❖ Trips away for top performers
- ❖ Regional incentives for top performers
- ❖ Company recognition-Globally

In addition to this every year the Pharmaceutical field magazine run an assessment day for candidates nominated by their customers as best representatives.

The day involves a series of role plays where the representatives are judged by customers in their therapy area of sales.

The prize is a national award of either primary care representative of the year, or a secondary care representative of the year, and a £1000 cheque. The recognition in the magazines and across the industry is great for your company and yourself.

Promotional Prospects

The majority of senior and middle managers in the industry have started their careers as medical representatives. The competition for advancement is therefore intense. However, those representatives with high sales achievements, together with management potential and a desire to progress in this direction, will be helped and encouraged to do so.

In addition to this some of the big companies offer international positions, or the opportunity to do 6month or 12month sabbaticals out in another country. This is an excellent offer for those who want to broaden their work experience in this industry.

These days there are other promotional roles working in the marketing department as product managers or medical education managers, for the medical department as medical liaison officers /medical science managers, or as field coaches or training managers for the training department, so advancement is excellent in this career.

16. Useful links and references

- www.allaboutmedicalsales.com

- www.pharmacareers.co.uk

- www.pharmafield.co.uk

- www.pfawards.co.uk

- www.pharmatimes.com

- www.hmprisonservice.gov.uk

- www.shldirect.com

- www.planitplus.net

- www.abpi-career.org.uk

- www.abpi.org

- www.nhs.uk

- www.dh.gov.uk

- www.pharmafile.com

- o www.inpharma.com

- o www.prospects.ac.uk

- o www.ukmedicalsalesjobs.co.uk

- o www.o2medical.com

- o ABPI, Code of Practice for the Pharmaceutical Industry, 2008.

- o Peel M, Successful Presentation in a week, Institute of management.

17. Recruitment Company Information

ROYCE CONSULTANCY	PHARMAFORCE
16 Melville Street Edinburgh EH3 7NS Tel: 01344 601144 Email:Royce.jobs@roycecons ultancy.com www.royceconsultancy.com	'CHILWELL' Dorton Road Chilton. Bucks HP18 9NB. Tel: 01844 202010 www.pharmaforce.co.uk
THE VACANCY **MANAGEMENT GROUP** 10 Market Square Alton. Hampshire GU34 1HD. Tel: 01420 82202 Email:action@vacancymgt.com www.vacancymgt.com	**ZENOPA** The Three Pines Church Road Penn Bucks HP10 8EG Tel: 01494818000 Email:enquiries@zenopa.com www.zenopa.com

TALENTMARK	SSC
Vintage House 37 Albert Embankment Vauxhall London SE17TL Tel: 08450952626 Email@talentmark.com www.talentmark.com	Ormond House 26-27 Boswell Street London WC1N 3JZ Tel: 02072424266 Email:enquiries@sscrecruitment.com www.sscrecruitment.com
ASHFIELD IN 2 FOCUS	**IHS**
Ashfield House Resolution Road Ashby de la Zouch Leicestershire LE65 1HW Tel: 08708501234 Email: enquiries@ashfieldin2focus.com www.ashfieldin2focus.com	15 Stafford St Edinburgh EH37BR Tel: 08450 6141 31 Email: kdarlison@ihs-ssc.com www.i-hs.co.uk

CHASE RECRUITMENT	NORTH 51
Suite A 6 Quayside Mills Edinburgh EH6 6EX Tel: 0131 553 6644 Email: recruit@chasepharmajobs.com www.chasepharmjobs.com	Biocity Nottingham Pennyfoot St Nottingham NG1 1GF Tel:01159503999 Email:contact@north-51.com www.north-51.com
STAR MEDICAL	CARROT PHARMARECRUITMENT LTD
Star House 4 Kelso Place Upper Bristol Road Bath BA1 3AU. Tel: 01255336335 Email: soloutions@starmedical.co.uk www.starmedical.co.uk	Pentland House Village Way Summerfields. Wilmslow Cheshire SK92GH Tel: 01625 541031 Email: enquiries@carrotpharma.co.uk www.carrotpharma.co.uk

www.ingramcontent.com/pod-product-compliance
Lightning Source LLC
Chambersburg PA
CBHW060621200326
41521CB00007B/848